JONAH AND THE WHALE

D1313950

ISBN: 1-56173-719-4

Contributing Writer: Marlene Targ Brill

Consultant: David M. Howard, Jr., Ph.D.

Cover Illustration: Stephen Marchesi

Book Illustrations: Gary Torrisi

David M. Howard, Jr., Ph.D. is an associate professor of Old Testament
and Semitic Languages, and is a member of the Society of Biblical
Literature and the Institute for Biblical Research.

Publications International, Ltd.

The people who lived in Nineveh were making God very unhappy. They had forgotten about God and what He wanted them to do. God wanted to send a message to the people. He chose Jonah, an Israelite, to be his messenger.

God said to Jonah, "Go to the city of Nineveh. Tell the people they have made me angry with their wicked ways. Tell them I will punish them."

The idea of doing this made Jonah afraid. He knew he had heard the voice of God. Yet, he didn't want to make the long trip to Nineveh. He was frightened because the people there were enemies of the people of Israel.

Rather than doing as God had asked, Jonah decided to hide. "I must find a place where God won't find me," Jonah thought. He packed some food and money and started out for Joppa. Joppa was a busy city in the opposite direction from Nineveh. Jonah hoped he could hide among the people of Joppa.

When he reached the bustling city, he became afraid again. "God will find me here and punish me," he worried. "I must go farther away." Jonah thought and thought about where to go. Then he noticed a ship.

"I know what I must do," he said. "I will take this ship across the sea to Tarshish. Surely, God will not find me there."

Jonah paid for his ticket and got on the ship. Tired from the long journey, Jonah went down into the cabin of the ship. He found a comfortable place to lay down and fell asleep. A short time later, the captain ordered the ship to leave the harbor. He looked at the blue sky overhead. The day was perfect for sailing.

Once they were out to sea, however, the sky changed greatly. A large storm swept over the sea. A strong wind rocked the boat. The rolling sea threatened to break the ship apart. The sailors were afraid. They threw the ship's cargo into the sea. They hoped a lighter ship would make it through the storm.

The danger did not go away. Each man prayed to his god. In spite of their prayers, the raging storm continued. The captain rushed to Jonah. "Get up," he ordered. "What are you doing asleep? Call on your God. Perhaps your God will keep us from dying."

The sailors above shouted to one another, "Someone has brought this storm upon us." They decided to cast lots (which was like drawing straws) to see who was causing all the problems.

When they cast the lots, it became clear that Jonah was responsible for all the trouble they were having. Everyone had questions for him.

"Why did you bring this storm?" asked the captain. "Where are you from? Who are your people?" Jonah answered, "I am a Hebrew from the land of Israel." Then Jonah explained that he was running away from God. The men were even more afraid. "What shall we do to quiet the sea?"

Jonah now realized there was nowhere to hide from God. So he told the sailors to throw him into the sea. "Then the sea will quiet down for you," he said.

The sailors didn't want to throw Jonah overboard. So they tried everything to bring the ship back to land. But the winds were too strong. Finally, they picked Jonah up and threw him into the sea.

At once, the winds stopped blowing. The sea stopped raging. The sky brightened. The sailors thought of Jonah and thanked God for their safety.

But Jonah was safe. God had sent a mighty fish to swallow him. Jonah lived in the belly of the fish for three days and three nights. During this time, Jonah prayed to God. He thanked God for letting him live. God heard Jonah's prayers and gave the large creature a command. The fish swam close to shore, opened its great mouth, and tossed Jonah out onto dry land.

Jonah heard the voice of God a second time. "Get up and go to Nineveh. Give the people my message." This time Jonah did as God commanded.

Jonah traveled a long time until he reached the busy city of Nineveh "In forty days God will destroy Nineveh," Jonah cried. He repeated these words again and again.

The people of Nineveh believed God. They were afraid for their city. Many stopped eating and wore rough rags to show God they were sorry.

God's words reached the king of Nineveh. He rose from his throne, took off his royal robes, and put on rough rags. Then the king sat in ashes. The king ruled that every person and animal should go without food and water. They were to stop behaving in their evil ways. They were to pray to God to forgive them so Nineveh could be saved.

God heard their prayers. The people stopped their evil ways. God forgave them and saved their city. The people rejoiced. Only Jonah was unhappy. Why had God made him travel all this way only to change His mind? "This is what I was afraid would happen," cried Jonah. "You are a good and forgiving God."

"Is it right for you to be angry?" asked God. Jonah did not answer. He left the city. After walking for a while, he sat down and looked toward the city's east wall. He waited to see what would happen next.

God caused a vine to grow over Jonah. The plant shaded Jonah from the burning sun. Jonah was very happy about the vine and the shade it gave him.

Early the next morning, God sent a worm to attack the vine. The strong branches drooped. Its leaves fell to the ground. Jonah awoke to find his beloved plant withered. He was confused over what happened to the plant. Then he noticed an ugly worm crawling on a branch. Jonah knew that God sent the worm. He became angry.

Once again, the sun beat down on the earth. Only this day there was no vine to give shade for Jonah's head. He was so faint he asked God to let him die.

But God said to Jonah, "Is it right for you to be angry about the vine?" "Yes," replied Jonah. "I am angry enough to die."

"You loved this vine that you did not grow. It was only on earth one day," said God softly. "Yet, you want me to destroy Nineveh. I cared for this great city and its people and animals over many years."

Jonah listened carefully. He now understood that God loves and forgives all people who turn to him. It doesn't matter who they are or where they are from.